nice!

YOU Deserve

hello

belongs to: ______

Made in the USA
Monee, IL
14 November 2021

82084372R00061